# REALLY, NURSE!

# *Really,*

# NURSE!

*Hundreds of nursing 'howlers' taken from the actual examination papers of many great hospitals*

ROGER BROOK

*did the compilation*

JACQUELINE MORAN

TIMOTHY BIRDSALL

*did the drawings*



JAVELIN BOOKS

POOLE · DORSET

First published in the UK 1962 and 1966 by Souvenir Press Ltd.
This Javelin Books edition first published 1985 by
Javelin Books, Link House, West Street, Poole, Dorset, BH15 1LL



ISBN 0 7137 1698 3

**British Library Cataloguing in Publication Data**

Brook, Roger
Really nurse! : howlers from nursing exam papers.
1. English wit and humor 2. Nursing—
Anecdotes, facetiae, satire, etc.
I. Title
827'.914'080355 PN6231.N9/

ISBN 0-7137-1698-3



Printed and bound in Great Britain by Hazell Watson & Viney Limited,
Member of the BPCC Group, Aylesbury, Bucks.

## A Word from the Compiler

They say that patients fall in love with their nurses. That may be just as well, if this book is any sign of what nurses are liable to do to their patients.

The 'howlers' which follow were all taken from the written answers to nursing examination papers. And let me be the first to admit that such a collection is jolly unfair. We all know what 'exam nerves' are like; when these follow upon months of trying to study each day after long gruelling hours on the ward, who can be surprised at whatever happens? I am a doctor myself and I know.

But unfair or not, no one will appreciate the 'howlers' more than nurses themselves. For a keen sense of humour is one of the first attributes of the perfect nurse. She must also possess unending patience, encyclopædic memory, exemplary tact, unshakeable calm, inexhaustible energy, incorruptible ethics, saintly temper, impeccable grooming, infallible judgement, sunny disposition, good looks, legible handwriting and no use for money or leisure. Is it any wonder that in the whole length and breadth of the land no such little angel exists? Except, of course, to her patients.

## Contents

## *On the Ward*

A question should be thoroughly red before it can be understood.

*The eye should roll around the face whilst it is being irrigated.*

The eye can be cleaned with a swat.

*The child vomited a large amount of blood at 7 p.m., mother coming up later.*

A pair of bowels on the trolley top would do to receive the equipment.

*The bowls are opened with a little suppository.*

The body is left for one hour before laying it out in order that it may become a stiff.

*The Matron must endeavour at all times to be a lady, although we all know how difficult this must be for her.*

The patient was nursed on an inferior sprung mattress.

*The child should never be left, this is only right.*

The marks are collected, washed, and boiled before being distributed daily.

Witch nurse must sign the drug register before the injection is given.

*The patient lies flat in bed, one small pillar being placed under her neck.*

As the patient walks down the ward be sure to notice his gate.

*The specimens are examined with the aid of a microscope and doctor in the lavatory.*

The Deputy Matron is a person who will hold the fort while the Matron is doing time.

*To prevent bed sores, an air ring may be used, another method is to fill the bed with water.*

The soreness of the patient's throat was eased with a gargoyle.

*The injection should be given in the upper outer hydrant of the patient's buttocks.*

Mattresses must have a good covey.

*The bed clothes should be turned down to the patient's waste.*

The Night Sister is responsible for waking the patient so that his sleeping drug can be given.

*The nurse should cheek with the sister, this will ensure no mistake is made with the dosage.*

Masks should be worn by the nurse to afford the patient some protection from her.

*Sister sent nurse to the curate to obtain some hypodermic needles.*

The Hospital comedian was quite a chaplin in his way.

*Sister and nurse were co-operating in an endeavour to make a really good report.*

The patient was flushed thus ensuring that water was given freely.

*A sandbog was placed at the patient's feet.*

The patient's four heads were bathed in sweat.

*The patient woke up in the morning with bogs under his eyes.*

Nurse warned the bed pans in the sluice before handing them out to the patients.

*The ward sister had the reputation of being a battle ox.*

Junior nurses were warned to give nothing sugared, the patient being a diabolic.

*Theatre sisters must have special peculiar qualities in order to stand their gory work day after day.*

The patient should be put into bed with an oxygen cylinder and a post anæsthetic tray, but take the hot water bottles out first.

*A record should be played of the patient's temperature, pulse, and respiration.*

Between them the doctor and the Almoner can do much to arrest the patient's mind.

*A member of the Management Committee said that in his opinion three months in the Preliminarv Training School was far too long, twelve weeks in his view was quite adequate.*

The patient was told to restrict his cigarette smoking to fifty after each meal.

*The dally woman will sweep and dust before breakfast.*

*The nurse agreed that she was well taut by that particular ward sister.*

There are many ways of removing sutures but it is best to use the right one.

*It is best to clean the patient's back with toe and then apply a cream.*

Matron called upon her Deputy to join her in a round.

Sister's standing was lowered in every patient's eye when she admitted she had no Red Cross qualifications.

*The patient was placed on the stretcher with his arms folded in his chest.*

The syringes were sterilised in the hot air department of the Laboratory.

*Cross infection and strangulation by red tape are responsible for a very high mortality rate in hospitals today.*

If a patient has worries the Almoner is just the person to elevate them.

*With few exceptions no patient should be confined in bed before operation.*

The patient going to theatre may obtain a comfit from the nurse going with her.

*The patient's face was noticed to be a little pail.*

The Matron tried to conceal her presents on the ward.

*The patient should be made to cough up, if he does not, he must be tipped up.*

To instil drops into a patient's eye pull out the lower lid and then put the drops in the exposed sack.

*The flannel is placed in a ringer and boiling water is then poured over.*

A soft sap is used to bath this patient.

*Next wash the patient's groins and genial organs, before doing the legs.*

Sputum cartoons may be used instead of mugs.

*A special basket takes the linen to the laundry, and she must make sure it is counted first.*

The patient is asked to take a breath through his mouth and then swallow the tub.

*The inhalation was given to the patient so that his respiratory tract could be disinfested.*

Olive oil is injected into the rectum using a tube and funnel, nurse will follow this later along with a soap and water enema.

*Emesses is the emptying of the stomach contents.*

The Sister complained that the fowl was being allowed among the clean laundry.

*The patient's legs were halved by a divided bed.*

While blanket bathing a patient, keep a sharp watch for rushes, marks, and pimps.

*The patient should be instructed to breathe an inhaler through the mouth and expel it through the nose.*

The patient's position in bed must be charged every two hours.

*The Assistant Matron as the name implies assists now and again during the week.*

After a motion was passed during the nurses' meeting, the Chairman thought it best to end the proceedings.

*The meeting was opened by the Chairman greeting the ladies, also the Matron.*

The Matron should be a woman whose heart is in the right place.

*If dust is created in the ward the patients may become sceptic cases.*

When dressing a wound a nurse must be very careful to swap it from within outwards.

*The nurse was shown how to put a bondage on the patient.*

The patient was admitted with bad corn on one foot.

*The patient objected when the nurse informed him she was going to take down his particulars.*

The nurse took great care to clean out the naval base on the patient's abdomen before his abdominal operation.

*The patient's hare was carefully wrapped in a triangular bandage.*

The nurse produced two robber catheters for the entry.

*The splint should be padded to prevent pressure on bonny prominences.*

Gum elastic catheters may be sterilised in a formal cabinet for six hours.

*A soap and water enema is an awfully common treatment.*

Use should be made of gutter percher to sit over the cotton wool.

*The patient was taught to get about on his crutch.*

Owing to the excessive shaking of blankets the air was full of staphylococks.

*The nurse put the lower leg in a backside splint.*

The patient's visitors were indeed difficult to bare.

*The nurse should use some tacks when dealing with apprehensive patients.*

A mustard plaster can be made by mixing mustard with flowers.

*A beer suction cup can be used with success.*

The temperature may be taken under the patient's tongs.

*Sister soon put the patient in his plaice.*

*The nurse can make a naked examination of the specimen before reporting to the ward sister.*

If the patient cannot pass urine, the simplest remedy is to turn his tap on so that he can hear it.

*A patient specimen was labelled and taken to the laboratory.*

The patient's arm was slung, with the hand going higher than the elbow.

*The nurse stated that after three years general training she would be a mental nurse.*

The patient insisted on having a bed pain whilst the visitors were in the ward.

*The patient is in grave danger if his nurse is not sterile.*

The best treatment for shock is to rape the patient in old blankets, making sure she is not overheated.

*The woman should have blankets under and over her, but onlookers must be kept outside.*

The patient must adhere closely to the bed rest.

*When bathing a baby it must be in a place free from droughts.*

The ice bag is applied to the head, and this is attached to the bed rail.

*Heat the bowels with boiling water and then empty them out.*

An infectious patient is nursed behind an invisible barrier which must not be moved.

*Sister instructed the senior nurse to go round and inspect all the patient's drains.*

Artificial restoration may help the patient to recover.

*If a person swallows an irritant poison the alimentary track will be inflames.*

The nurse must never be instructed to apply the tourniquet over the patient's bear skin.

## *All in the Mind*

An introvert is a person who is drawn into a shell.

*For group therapy to succeed there must be intimacy between Psychiatrists, nurses, and patients.*

There are not many G.P.I.'s seen now, large doses of penicillin soon puts an end to them.

*In most mental hospitals there is a great shortage of certified staff.*

To really understand a mentally disturbed patient the nurse must project herself inside the patient's brain.

*Schizophrenia is often referred to as split personality. This means the patient is split into two distinct halves.*

# The Body Beautiful

Wax glands in the ear protect the organ from foreigners.

*The pupil is nothing more than a whole in the eye. In some people it is big, in others small, but unless you have been peculiarly born it is there in some size or another.*

The stomach is covered with a serious membrane.

*The stomach is supplied by an involuntary nerve called the pneumatic.*

The ærta is a long tub whose contents are very precious to the body.

*The eye is the organ of site, the sight of which is in a holler in the temple.*

At the back of the eye one may see a retinue.

*The heart is the only organ in the body made of heart muscle.*

The heart is a muscular organ like a human pump, which pumps the heart around the body at regular intervals.

*The heart is an organ the shape of a heart. It is not quite heart shaped because there are tubes protruding from it, four from top left, an umbrella handle from bottom left, a 'Y' shaped connection from bottom right and two tubes from top right.*

The brain will soon become a weekend one.

*At the back of the throat are two long pillars of faeces.*

The mouth is situated in the lower part of the face and it is known as a buckled cavity.

*The diaphragm is a doom shaped muscle.*

The nurse must possess the patient's full corporation if she is to gain his confidence.

*The patient may be sand-bagged to prevent her slipping down the bed.*

The large intestine is continuous with a bag called secombe.

*There are 5,000,000 red blood corpuscles in 1 cubic millimetre of male blood, and owing to their many peculiarities women have fewer.*

The human body is covered with mussels, some of which we can move when we want to, others we can't.

*The stomach is jay shaped when it is empty.*

An eye is kept on the patient's chest.

*The blood vessels have 3 intimate coats.*

The male organ of degeneration is called a penis.

*The large intestine terminates at the anus where it is guarded by a spinster.*

Micturition is the art of passing urine.

*The knee joint is very loose in its behaviour.*

The heart is situated between the two lugs.

*The lungs are contained in the pleural sacks.*

Blood is returned from the head by the Juggler vein.

*The patient was able to breathe in air but could not expire quick enough.*

The suprarenal glands are situated up the poles of the kidneys.

*The œsophagus is a long tin tube which connects the pharynx with the stomach.*

The tube in the neck is known as the trackear.

*A structure called the cockleer in the ear allows us to hear.*

The bacteria are imprisoned in white cells when they are caught.

*The kidneys are situated outside the perineum.*

The vertebræ in the small of the back are known as lumber.

*The sublingual glands are the smallest pears in the mouth.*

There are two plates forming the roof of the mouth, one is hard, the other soft.

*The knee joint contains some very special cartridges.*

Owing to the difference in structure of the vocal chords, a woman's voice is heard very often as a shrill sound, as compared with the base sounds emitted by the male.

*As most men cannot have babies their pelvices are somewhat rigid compared with child-bearing females.*

From the kidneys lead two ducks; these find their way into the bladder.

*Three vassels communicate with the bladder.*

The function of the kidney is to rid the body of its waist.

*The fluid flows from the kidney to a part called Henley where much water is reabsorbed.*

The inside of the kidney is full of callouses.

*Each kidney contains 5,000,000 tubercles in a normal person.*

Urine is avoided through the urethra.

*The collectors in the kidney extract valuable substances from the body and then run to the Pyramids.*

Respiration is when the patient breathes in and then expires.

*The large intestines are in the elementary track.*

*At the lower part of the vertebral column one will find the cocksits.*

Teeth are made of enamel and need calcium to prevent them becoming chipped.

*Lack of vitamin E which is known as the antisterility vitamin results in the female producing eggs without yolks.*

Deafication is the art of passing fæces into the rectum.

*As the fluid passes through the large intestines it leaves a mass behind in a more concencrated form.*

The faces go slowly down the intestines finally leaving through the anal exit.

*The large intestine starts at the colic valve.*

The walls of the small intestines are lined with villas.

*The best room for eye trouble is one which is well alight.*

*Without a heart we would not be here, so we should pay our respects to it.*

The rate of the heart beat can be felt by felling the radial artery at the wrist.

*There are two important factors in the blood called ANTIGENTS A & B.*

A potion of the fifth cranial nerve supplies all the muscles which direct eating.

The ear is the organ of earing.

*In life a person has three sets of teeth:*

(*a*) *Temporary.*
(*b*) *Permanent.*
(*c*) *False.*

The nerve supply to the lungs is vague.

# *Keeping it Clean*

*The shopkeeper should thoroughly rap all cakes before selling them to make sure all disease is eliminated.*

Food should not be picked up by hand but with tongues.

*Clean overalls or trousers should be worn to polish the fruit on.*

These are some of the types that help in hygiene of the country:

(1) Road sweepers.
(2) Dustmen.
(3) Nurses on the district and so on.

All these add up to the answer, prevention of spread.

*If blue bottles come through the larder window trouble is around.*

Cooks should be trained to wash their hands after a visit to the toilet; it is through wiping them on food that diseases are spread.

Flies may be shot down whilst in flight by the aid of D.D.T. bombs.

*Overcrowding is not necessary. People when they get married, their parents say they can live with them until they get a house built. Some people think, well as long as we can live with them it is allright. BUT IT IS NOT. After they have been married a few months they start having children, these grow up and this goes on. Overcrowding then occurs, air is not allowed to enter, with too many in the bed diseases are caught. Conditions like this can be likened to the many hundreds of people who were put in a black hole in Calcutta and buried alive.*

Rest is essential if habits are to be good ones, if you do not rest then habits will be bad ones, so proper rest and good cleaning of the body will produce a nurse who can be relied upon to perform any old job the sister may have on her list.

*Our Tutor has stated that in her opinion all infection in hospitals is caused by dirty nurses, therefore personal hygiene and cleanliness is next to godliness, and is the first thing to remember if you want to prevent wounds from becoming pussy.*

The important thing in the maintenance of health is personal cleanliness. This commences when the person is getting up in the morning, and it continues until the person is ready for getting up again.

*You always find a person who does not practice personal cleanliness is not nice to be near.*

Everything about personal cleanliness should be kept very clean, making sure that the habits are not forgotten.

*The body needs a daily inspection to make sure every part is in proper working order.*

Hair should be bushed at least twice daily.

*A private maiden is an old fashioned type of closet.*

The teeth should be brushed with a brush and toothpaste. The best method is to have two brushes and keep one of them in a septic solution.

*Clothes should be well washed and ironed for hygienic conditions and also for decorating purposes.*

In bad light people may screw up their eyes and the damage they do may never be undone.

*Housewives when baking should wear the appropriate head gear.*

Flies may land on composed heaps then pass through a crack in a house, settle on persons within and cause trouble amongst them. Few escape this vital pest.

*If overcrowding continues water vapour increases and people will shout for air, this when heard denotes air hunger.*

We seek them here, we seek them there, we seek those horrid flies everywhere.

*Flies are abundant wherever rubbish, manure, filth and hospital food are found.*

Food should be kept covered in shops because of the diseased types who buy it.

*If open shoes are worn on duty the toe nails should be kept clean and short as they are on view to all the patients.*

Curt shoes and swede shoes are generally bared by the Matron.

*The Medical Officer of Health is responsible for the health of his own personal areas.*

The Local Authorities spend money raised by the local rats.

*As nurses are on their feet all day they should do away with their heels.*

The child depends for his earliest car on the midwife.

*An Almoner is an expert at finding out other people's business.*

If the patient is worried about his wife and family whilst he is in hospital the Almoner will probably be able to dispose of them for him.

*Cows and other poultry should not be allowed near the well otherwise the water may become contaminated.*

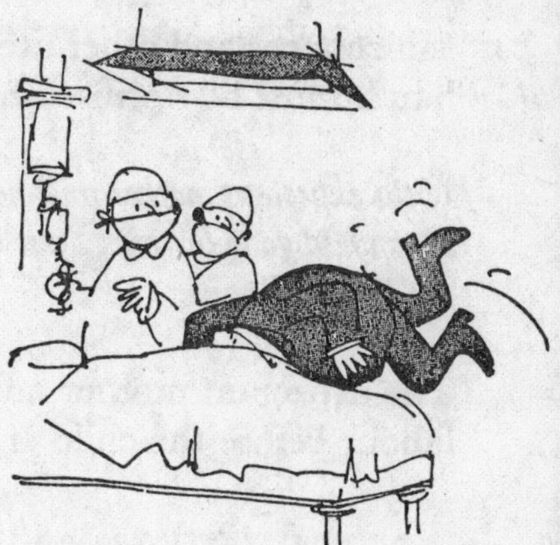

With electric fires in the home the only thing to be done is to switch on the currants.

*If a gas fire is used the occupants of the room would feel stuffed.*

Primary hæmorrhage occurs when the surgeon enters the patient's abdomen.

The midwife was proud to deliver the wife's first mail.

*If it were not for water, England during the last world war would not have been such a healthy place to live in.*

The Medical Officer of Health of his area notifies the Medical Officer of Health of the next area to be on the look out and so the word passes round.

*The cow's rudders must be thoroughly washed before milking.*

Milk churns and other utensils such as the milkers hands must be sterilised by boiling.

*If the expectant mother will not go to the ante-natal clinic she should go to her own doctor who after all is responsible for her condition.*

The expectant mother must be prepared for hard labour before the child is borne.

*A carrier is a person who slips a disease to someone else without that person knowing it.*

The nurse should keep her nails carefully paired.

*Local anæsthetics are used in miner surgery.*

Pure milk is obtained from cows who have been certified.

*Socks and stocks should be changed frequently.*

Oxygen helps to purify the water if algy is present in it.

*Water crept up the ribbon gauze by caterpillary attraction.*

The water seal in the pipe was there to trap backward floes.

The Health Visitor and the Almoner should be intimate if they are to work together; they usually maintain close contact by having weekly get togethers.

## Short Cuts to Surgery

The surgeon may order the bloody pressure to be taken.

*For a fractured thigh bone a skin tractor is often used to pull the broken bones apart.*

The patient was admitted with large buns on his face.

*The surgeon examined the patient's face and diagnosed a badly fractured jew.*

A malecot or butterfly emerged from a hole in the patient's abdomen.

*Empyema is present when the patient's pleura becomes distended with puss.*

The progress of the patient from her operation depended on the presence of a sucker.

*The patient was suspended in the Balkans.*

Stones were blocking the ducks and the patient turned yellow.

*If the patient in plaster is tight the nurse should try elevating.*

A plaster of paris splint for a fractured tibia will take six hours to dry, twenty-four hours to harden and three months to come off.

*After the surgeon has finished with the patient the physiotherapist will make the patient fit again.*

The woman was suffering from hammered toes.

*A complication after operation for hernia is orchiditis.*

Some surgeons have a change of character when they give their performance in the theatre.

*The surgeon ordered a hip spiker to be applied to the patient's leg.*

The patient had a semi-colonectomy for cancer of the large intestines.

*Syphilis is a venerable disease caused by a cork-screw called a treponema.*

The gonococcus may be lurking on a toilet seat for his next victim.

*Torticollis is also known as rye neck.*

In tetanus the wound must be exercised and irrigated with hydrogen peroxide solution.

*In tonsillitis the tonsils are always read.*

After appendicectomy the patient should be ambulance as soon as possible.

*The surgeon may do a colostomy on two stages.*

The pain was felt in the right iliac fossil.

*The baby was suffering from a cleft plate.*

A Napier's cup and stem pessary may be used for women with weekend vaginas.

*If surgical instruments were not sterilised, it would be like eating one's dinner with a very dirty garden fork.*

By approaching the kidney carefully from the patient's backside the peritoneal cavity is not entered.

*Canker of the bladder was diagnosed.*

Atropine is given before operation to dry up the patient's juices.

*Before the patient departs for the theatre he is given a bottle and he must empty his bladder into this.*

Nurse should ensure that all the public hairs are removed before patient goes to theatre.

*The results of this operation are good, the mortality rate being regarded as* highly *satisfactory.*

If the patient is to have a light spinal anæsthetic he is tipped head first.

*The young child with a fractured femur was hung from a gallows.*

The tetanus bacillis is a spoor forming organism.

*The patient was admitted to the Out-Patient Department with a cute face that required stitching.*

The patient was stitched with catsguts.

*The patient was admitted with prostrate trouble.*

The patient sustained a potty fracture of the ankle.

A car splint is applied to a colles fracture of the wrist.

*Penicillin was ordered as an umbrella to prevent infection from descending on the patient.*

The patient may slip and stain his ankle.

*A fracture is a brake in a bone.*

Heat is a physical gent used in treatment of both surgical and medical cases.

*In appendicitis the surgeon may press on the painful area and the pan will emerge on the other side of the abdomen.*

A fractured femur may be immobilised by using a splinter which is padded first to prevent it digging in the patient.

*The man was admitted to hospital suffering from a severe muscle strain which he said was caused by a wench.*

The patient should be given one table to suck before going to theatre, this will render the throat insensitive.

*If the fracture is compound titanic serum should be given.*

For fractured neck of femur plaster of Paris is applied from head to foot.

## *Test Tubes and Bed Pans*

In Korea the patient may throw himself about.

*The doctor will use a pal containing 1-20 carbolic to catch the fluid.*

If an aminophylline suppository is given before a breathless patient settles to sleep it will abort her.

*A patient suffering from acute nephritis may have a pain in the lion.*

Although the Physician and Surgeon could not agree the patient made good progress.

*If the patient is tapped below the knee it will reveal a jerk to the doctor.*

The patient's breath had a fœtus smell.

*Diabetic comma is a very serious sign.*

The response to cold varies from person to parson.

*The legs may show a tendency to smell on standing.*

The patient was comma toes.

*The child obviously had hooping cough.*

The child had chicken pox and her face had a number of peck marks upon it.

*If the physician does not like the case he will then call in the surgeon.*

The woman complained of pain in her left beast.

The incubation period is the time taken for the germs to hatch out their eggs.

*The doctor ordered the patient's stomach to be wished out and a specimen sent for inspection.*

A test dosage of the drug should be given first to prepare the patient for what is to come after.

*The patient suffering from gastric ulcer was told to avoid food containing pipes.*

The girl always got spring fever in the hay.

*A virus cannot be seen, only felt.*

The patient was given lent insulin to cover him for a longer period.

*The patient recovered in spite of treatment.*

The patient had no sensation in the skin below the coastal margin.

*Lumbar puncher is done to relieve headache.*

The patient should be boarded up for medicines by the doctor.

Owing to coughing the patient may become a little horse.

*The patient vomited the fowl infected contents of the small intestines.*

If the patient's breathing becomes very distressed he may be given an iron lung.

*The patient's head was growing very bold.*

The patient may have ticks of his face.

*Physical workers are unlikely to get coronary thrombosis; the mental ones do however, such as doctors.*

The patient was suffering from a decease which could not be cured.

*Rubella in pregnancy may cause the expectant mother to produce a baby with a whole heart.*

Boldness is caused because hairs lack food.

*The rubber tube was attached to the cannula so that the patient's abdomen could have no difficulty in draining into the bucket.*

The patient's teeth were covered with tata.

*A fictional test meal is a method of examining the stomach.*

In coronary thrombosis the severity of the attack depends upon the sight of the clot.

*The common cold is caused by an organism called the droplet bacillus.*

The doctor may try and simulate the patient by some means or other.

*In chronic nephritis a director is given to the patient to make her pass more urine.*

To clear sputum posterior drainage is carried out three times a day.

*A diabetic patient who is having insulin must be warned always to eat the fool diet allowed him.*

Thyrotoxicosis is a disease of women because it reveals an over emotional, talkative and irritating person.

*The patient's hips became waisted.*

The Physician ordered fluids to be given by a drip. His houseman was the obvious person to do this.

*No part of the patient should be bear until the doctor is ready to cope.*

The patient appeared to be in pain as he was throwing himself all over the beds.

*A characteristic of typhoid fever is the production of pea soup by the patient's bowels.*

The patient is given electric lights intravenously to replace those he has lost.

*The body requires two pints of water daily in order to perform its social functions.*

The doctor stated on the patient's case sheet that he had found rails in the patient's lungs.

*Acute rheumatism is noted for its panfull joints.*

The donor is made comfortable on a couch and his blood is then removed drop by drop until the doctor is satisfied.

*The transfusion service does not allow the donor to be cut down.*

Counter irritants are gents which irritate the tissues.

*The patient was suffering from shingle around his waist.*

*Cupping may be used to relieve the patient's deep seat pain.*

Epsom salts given first thing in the morning will move the patient quickly.

*Disorder of the suprarenal glands may result in a cushion disease.*

# *Once after Meals*

If the patient will not take his medicine by mouth it may be possible for the nurse to cox him.

*Before giving the medicine read and examine the labia three times carefully.*

Digitalis is obtained from a fox glove.

*Strychnine is obtained from a tree back.*

Morphia is derived from popeye seeds.

*Iron and a Copper is needed to make red blood corpuscles.*

When giving medicines place the cork in the crook's little finger whilst pouring out the dose.

*The patient will suffer from a steaming nose.*

*When certain drugs are being given to the patient his white blood must be examined.*

Castor oil may be given to loosen the patient up.

*A change of heart can be produced by giving digoxin.*

Drugs were given to dilute the patient's bronchioles.

*A nurse has to be able to work out doses of drugs; for this reason it is better for her to be an adder.*

A small doss is sufficient to settle the patient for the night.

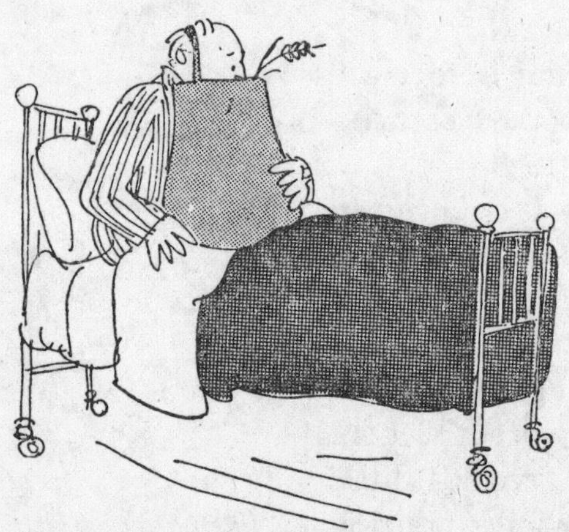

*A patient must be given a well balanced stable diet.*

*The doss for a child is smaller than that for an adult.*

Drugs taken by the moth may be in the form of powders or pills.

*The ear symptoms disappear when the doss is reduced.*

Suppositories are made of jellytin or cocoa.

*If largactil is used it will enable the patient to treat the hospital as a huge joke.*

# *Food for Thought*

The mother's milk is rich in certain vitamins, the amount depending on the pasture she is fed on.

*Fats are derived from animal and vegetable sauces.*

Sit the baby up in the middle of the feed and then brake his wind.

*The patient who was obeast had to go on a reducing diet.*

The patients were bed-panned before their meals.

*Make sure the patient is given plenty of calories, and they can be hard boiled or scrambled.*

In paralysis of the soft palate thickened fluids will be found easier to swallow than tin ones.

*Make sure the patient is given plenty of calories, and be sure you serve them up attractively.*

At first the diet consists of fluids, but when the patient is strong enough to face it, hospital diet can be given.

*The patient was given a wait-reducing diet before being discharged home to attend the out-patients department.*

Do not keep one eye on the clock whilst feeding a patient. Place them both on the patient and keep them there.

*The patient should have a slumming diet, said the doctor.*

An accurate wait record of the patient is essential, and this is often done in Out-Patients Department.

Men, being what they are, need more food than women.

*A pregnant housewife would I think need a slightly different diet to that of a normal human being.*

Before meals each patient is given a bedpan to improve his appetite.

## *(Very) Odd Jottings*

*The patient was given oxygenaire as he was cyanosed.*

The specimens were lined up in roes for the doctor's benefit.

*The patient's muscles should be thoroughly exorcised before his operation.*

Make sure the tuck is removed from the patient's bed before settling him down for the night.

*All patient's beds must be carefully striped before they are made.*

The nurse should never have a drag from an unmarked bottle.

*Dangerous drugs must be kept locked up with the ward sister.*

The baby is finished off after bathing her by putting gently.

*Ships are sent to the theatre and matron's office when the day of operation is fixed.*

Under the National Health Service matrons are becoming exstink.

*The swallowing of foreigners' bodies occurs particularly in young children.*

All urine which is past must be recovered for the doctor.

*The area of the chest to be operated on must be thoroughly rapped with sterile towels.*

The outside of the ear is known as a pinner.

*The tube should be run through by the nurse to expel the air.*

The course of the patient was charted for fourteen days.

*The patient complained of panes in his head.*

The surgeon restored the patient's airway by inserting a lobster tail through his windpipe.

*The surgeon decided to close the wound with a mattress.*

The patient had an epolitic fit.

*Perforation means that the ulcer has escaped from the patient's stomach.*

The woman attended the Ante Natal Clinic for relaxation exercises in order that she could enjoy her birthday.

*Baby's condition was diagnosed as hair lip.*

The two ends of the fractured bone were at first held together by a bloody clot.

*In Paget's disease the patient undoubtedly becomes a big head.*

The surgeon discovered that the patient had a quince in his throat.

*Getting rid of bed bugs from a house was formerly a major's operation.*

Nurse was sure she had an illegitimate excuse which would satisfy the Matron.

The eggs of the scabies mite hatch into lather within a few days.

*Smoke can be a serious treat to health.*

There are four peas situated in the neck of the parathyroid variety.

*Sensational fibres make the brain aware of what is going on around us.*

The patient was splaced on the bed with all but the public area uncovered.

*The eyelids blank every few seconds.*

The baby has two holes in his head covered with skin. These are termed the dardenelles.

*The mouth is a bonny cavity lined with atishoo.*

The nose communicates with a cavity called the antrum of Dartmoor.

*Among the bones which form the face are the two mailers.*

Women's brains are smaller than man's but they make up for this deficiency in other directions.

## *Eat, Drink and Be Merry*

For a test meal 2 tablespoonfuls of wheat are added to 1 quart of water and this is given to the patient after his stomach has been withdrawn with a syringe.

*Males eaten hurriedly are probably the cause of peptic ulceration.*

The patient said he knew he had indigestion badly because his heart was burning.

*A high fitty diet is thought likely to cause coronary thrombosis.*

The overweight patient was put on a very strict low silt diet.

*After the patient has had her male, she should be allowed to rest before the next one.*

The nurse should use all her natural wiles to tempt the patient to cooperate with her, particularly at mealtimes.

*The patient must be told to void any foodstuffs which bring on his symptoms.*

A good nourishing duet is also important to keep skin and tissues in good shape.

*Do not spoil the patient's nightware by dripping food on it.*

You should not try to push the patient with large amounts of food.

*The nurse must paws before she inserts the next mouthful into the patient.*

Sugar is essential if fits are to be used in the body.

*Vivacious eating is thought to predispose to peptic ulceration.*

*The patient was given an alight diet.*

Patient's with a tendency to gut should be advised to avoid articles of food rich in purines.

*The patient should avoid all matey foods and stick to milk.*

Dried fruits such as raisins also fags, should be avoided.

*The patient could have some battered toast for his early morning breakfast.*

The nurse should note whether the patient's ribs are sticking through her nightdress, if so she is emancipated.

He will be given a suit and nourishing diet during his stay in hospital.

*The patient's pate should not be overloaded with food.*

If the child does not have sufficient vitamin D, he will grow up with a tendency to rackets.

*Sister told the patient that as a special treat she would give him a nicely cooked stake for his lunch.*

If a hot male is sent up to the ward quick service will prevent cooling.

*The patient is given straw along with his drink.*

Proteins are responsible for replacing the wear and tar of tissues.

*The patient must be encouraged to drink plenty of coal fluids to help lower the temperature.*

The patient should have a feeding cap to help him with fluids.

*The doctor always orders the type of individual food for the patient, but it is the nurse's duty to see that the docter's orders are eaten.*

The patient did not look well, and said she felt offal.

*The patient should have easy excess to the food on his locker.*

## Danger, Nurse at Work

The buttocks must be brought in line with the hedge on the bed.

*Covered bowels on the trolley top will contain all the necessary ingredients to cover the wound.*

Mr. Smith can sit belt upright for his lumbar-puncture.

*The doctor carefully marks the area which is going to be punched, this is between the 4th and 15th lumbar vertebrae.*

The doctor worms his way through the vertebrae until he reaches the intrathecal space.

*The patient is pulled to the edge of the bed and his spine is then drawn to get it in position.*

The patient is admitted into a well wormed bed.

*Special core was given to the patient's pressure areas to harden the skin.*

The patient's hare was long and carried germs all over the ward.

*The patient's bad linen must never brush the floor.*

The nurse must scrub her hinds before she goes near the patient.

*The nurse will use an orange stuck with cotton wool to insert into the patient's nostrils for cleaning purposes.*

Edward Tudor's spectacles are used for giving oxygen to the patient.

*The nurse should wash the fete twice daily.*

If the hair is arranged in tidy plants, it will do much to improve the patient's appearance.

*The patient's hands must be moved so that the muscles do not loose their power.*

If the patient's head is examined and found to be nutty, the nurse can use vinegar to loosen and cure the trouble.

*The patient if he is able to understand is then told what is going to happen to him, if he does not understand then it does not matter what the nurse does to him.*

It is essential that the patient's fingers and toes should be kept tidy and in place.

*A dirty nurse will help the sterile nurse to do the dressings, but she is not allowed near the patient or she may act as a vendor of infection.*

Soiled dressings are placed in buns, these are then handed out to the porters.

*The patient's fingers should be trimmed to shape before her blanket bath.*

Sandbags could be used to prevent the patient's feet from becoming draped.

*Nurses should not cling to the sheets when making a patient's bed, as this gives the germs an opportunity to crawl on her apron.*

A ring will prevent the patiens getting sores on her soul.

*The cublicles on the patient's nails should be pushed down gently.*

The patient is washed all over with warm soupy water.

*When taking the patient's pulse the nurse should note the number of beaks and record them on the chart.*

The patient should first be looked over for signs of defamities.

*Female patients can see their hands, male patients do not bother, therefore a perfumed hand lotion will help.*

The nurse did not like the dirty jab she was given by sister in the sluice.

*The nurse should always wear her musk whilst attending to the patients.*

The hands of a patient should always be washed after the use of a bed pin.

*If the nurse is wise, she will never let a patient take advantage of her, matron will not help her if this happens.*

Shock can be foetal so care must be taken of the patient whilst she is in this condition.

*The patient should be encouraged to move his hands all over the bed to prevent hand drop.*

If a phony was handy I would get in touch with the surgeon at once.

*The nurse must make sure her mast is satisfactory before she ventures to do the patient's dressing.*

Usually the patients who come into hospital are not used to lying in bed all the time, and if they are made to, their morality drops and this does not aid the patient's recovery.

*On taking the patient's pulse, nurse found it to be string.*

When the nurse puts the gown on, it should be inside out and when she hangs it up afterwards it should be outside in.

*The bedpan is mapped after use.*

The patient will probably have disposable tishoos.

*The heels are a potential sight for pressure sores.*

The nurse is responsible for the filing of hot water bottles and she should repeat this performance every 4 hours.

*If a child is in a steam tent, it is not right that he should be left.*

If the patient's heels are read, the nurse will probably see a warning re bedsores.

*When moving Mrs Smith, nurse should grasp the other nurses arm and carry it to the foot of the bed.*

The best sight for an intramuscular injection is undoubtedly the buttocks.

*The sterile pick is placed on the top shelf of the trolley ready for use on the patient's wound.*

The trolley tap must be washed with soap and water before anything else is done.

*The patient may complain of being sour if he lies in one position for too long.*

The child had a look like pane on her face.

*Look at the patient carefully when he is admitted to make sure there are no scares present.*

The patients may be kept awake by just one nosy patient on the ward.

*The patient should have something to do or he will become board.*

Every effort should be made to prevent the patient from obtaining bedsores.

*After staff nurse has signed for the drugs she must be sure to lick them away carefully.*

*The patient was kept in bed until improvement was noted.*

The treatment consists of robbing the patient's areas with the hands.

*The patient may complain of not having any energen, and therefore a very long period of convalescence is required.*

The breathing could be sighing due to hare hunger.

*The doctor inserted a needle into the spain to draw off C.S.F.*

The best position for lumbar puncture is to have the patient curled up like a bull.

*The best position to nurse the hemiplegic patient is in the semi prawn position.*

A heal pad is placed under the leg to aid its recovery.

*The whole of the lag is to be shaved before the procedure.*

After wishing, the feet should be carefully dried.

*A bed cradle is used to take the weight of the bedclothes off the patient's upper lugs.*

Mental crystals can be added to the inhaler as an inducement.

*The patient was a little bugger compared with his size a year previously.*

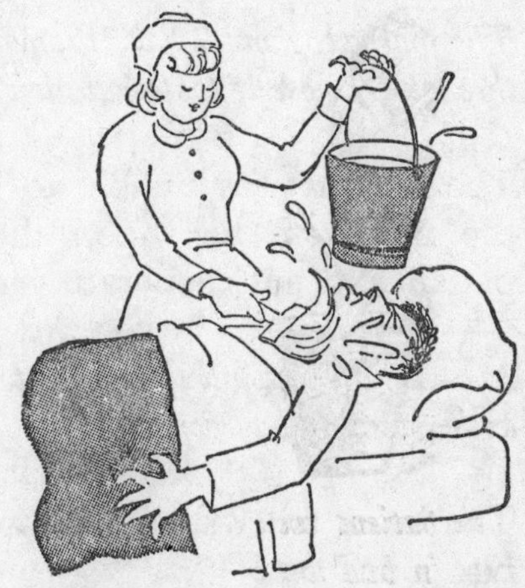

*A pint brush may be used for applying lotion to the throat.*

The patient should put her head over the jug, take deep breaths and inhale it.

*The patient should have a sputum pit by his bedside and he will usually fill this during postural drainage.*

The patient who has diarrhoea should be barricade nursed.

*If the patient is kept in bed too long he will not circulate well, and thrombosis could be his lot.*

A cork bunk is placed in the inhaler before the patient has it.

*The patient should hail through the mouth and out through the nose if the inhalation is to be effective.*

The patient was unable to go to the toilet, so the nurse sat her upon the bed pin, but the patient did not cooperate very well.

*Mrs. Smith's mouth to let has to be dealt with as soon as her visitors had departed.*

The heart failer should be nursed in an upright position.

*The hair would be tiddly braided by the nurse.*

I would keep up his morale by having him shaved by the hospital barker.

*If contact is made with such a parson, a full bath to which a disinfectant has been added should be taken as soon as possible.*

Watch that the patient does not become a little tyre when she is got up for the first time.

*To prevent infection hair should be kept off colour and away from the face.*

The patient was given oxygen using naval tubes which were passed along the base.

*The patient complained of chipped arms and hands, and was given a hand cream to improve matters.*

*The needle should be driven into the tissues by an angel of about 45 for a subcutaneous injection.*

It was decided that an ice bog might relieve the patient's headache and fever.

The temperature was high and the patient's face was flashing.

*The patient was hot and flushed and kept complaining of first.*

A builder is placed over the patient's stump to stop it from jumping about the bed.

*The nurse should stand behind the patient and irritate the eye from within outwards.*

A light male is given at 6 p.m. and then nothing by mouth until after the test.

*The nurse must keep her nails closely paired and her skin should not become sore and crocked.*

Occupational therapy is given to keep the patient hoppy and contented.

*In the knee chest position the patient rusts on knees, arms, and chest.*

A fomentation is a method of applying mist heat and is as a rule applied 4 hourly.

*Mrs. Church's licker should be within easy reach of her without her having to reach for it.*

The patient is told to ring her bell for the nurse if she fancies a drunk.

*The nurses would then lift Mr. Smith down the bed using the Australian lift, being careful to make sure his feet were not hanging off over the edge of the bed.*

The clean sheets would then be rolled under the patient and tacked in all around the bed.

*The nurse should notice whether Mrs. Brown developed a rush after having the medicine.*

The wait of the patient should be recorded on entering the hospital, and then at intervals.

*The patient may be nursed on a rippling mattress to prevent sores forming.*

I would observe whether he was swearing, hot or cold, and then decide whether to tepid sponge or not.

*The nurse should do the pressure areas thoroughly, and make sure the annual region is kept clean and free from soreness.*

A specimen of urine is obtained for ward tasting.

*The patient should never be led down in the bed if he is breathless.*

The bed is neatly stripped and the patient covered with a worm blanket.

*A good nurse is a curtain nurse when dealing with drugs, otherwise she is a menass.*

The nurse should not treat her elderly patient's like simpletons. They are always much more intelligent than the nurses looking after them these days.

*The patient should always have a ball so that she can attract the nurse's attention when she wants anything.*

The pain killing drug which has been made up in liquid foam can be given by mouth or by injection.

*Mrs. Jones bed would be clanged from top to bottom to make her feel fresh and comfortable.*

The pressure areas must be dyed and powdered frequently to prevent sores forming.

*Mr. Smith must be nursed with great care because of his falling heart.*

The patient must always be in a position which places least stain on the heart.

*The student nurse must always report to the train nurse or her sister when going on and off duty.*

The patient should be told to adopt a laxative position when sitting on the bedpan.

*The nurse must also observe the position of the patient's limbs, and make sure that no listing deformities result from her neglect.*

The patient was nursed in Fowler's position, but would keep slapping down the bed.

*The cradle was placed over the patient's legs to prevent foot drip.*

Patients must be encouraged to drink plenty of coal fluids to help lower the temperature.

*The patient should be nursed in the semi cucumbent position for best results.*

A buck rest is useful to keep the patient upright.

*The patient should be able to open her drawers without placing strain on her heart.*

The top of the file is removed and the rest of it is then injected into the patient making sure he gets it all.

*If the patient is obese, the nurse should certainly put her eye on him.*

All this patient's fluids should be placed on a fluid cart together with all her urine and faeces.

*All many patients want to do on admission to hospital is to be a liar in bed all day.*

After attending to the patient, the nurse goes to the ball and washes her hands.

*The nurse should use every measure she can think of to promote bed sores in her patients.*

The patient's weight should be recorded at the entrance to the hospital and weekly thereafter.

*Any linen with tares in it should be taken out of circulation.*

The rubber tubing from the oxygen cylinder goes to a wolf.

*The nurse takes the soiled sheets from the bed and places them in the linen ship.*

The bed is made on the top part of the patient first and then the nurses work round to his bottom.

*If the patient breathes through his mouth he will be perched.*

If the patient is nursed flat, be careful he does not swallow his tong.

*The patient's bet is made each morning with two nurses.*

The patient should be nursed on a nipple mattress.

*The patient should have a sputum carton on his locker, because he is always expecting sputum.*

The patient will do better if he is nursed in a three quarter prune position.

*The patient was fat, and this was obviously due to ademon.*

All the pillows not actually required should be placed on a char at the side of the bed.

*The patient is lifted down the bed by an Australian if she is breathless.*

After the enema a pun should be offered to the patient.

*All the soiled linen from the bed should be placed in billy carrier.*

The patient should be treated as a hole and not just her ulcer.

*If the adult in hospital is a child, he may miss his parents.*

Not only does the patient's physical condition deteriorate, but also their spiritual condition. They become very depressed and are aggressive and very often crawl in a little shell from which they often do not emerge from for days, and this retards their physical condition.

*Nurse remembering her lectures on nurse/patient relationship and tried beyond endurance by a particularly difficult patient, lost her control at last and flung at him "Oh you, you, human being".*

When a patient has been in the ward for a long time, it is to be expected that the nurses will be happily related to him.

*The patient should be given national health service treatment except when he is in a private room.*

## *Cleanliness is Next to Godliness*

If the patient is found to be suffering from poison an anecdote should be found as soon as possible.

*The patient was lifted and transfixed to the ambulance.*

If the patient is bleeding from the leg, press your thumb firmly in her groan.

*If Johny has swallowed tablets, first aid treatment is to make him sick and give them back.*

The methods of respiration which would be used are mouth to moth, and an alternative is trafalgar nelson's method.

*Mouth to mouth breathing—You then remove your mouth from the patient's and allow her to expire gently away.*

Silver vests method will often restore the patient's breathing to normal.

*If the patient breaks a leg, it should be strapped with the other to keep it still.*

If cardiac arrest is to be treated a large bard is placed in the patient's bed.

*A first aider should do fast things first.*

If a tourniquet is applied to this patient, you must not forget to place a tee on his head.

*The mouth to mouth breathing tube goes down to the anal pharynx.*

A clover hitch sling was used to rest the patient's arm.

*Comprehensive haemorrhage may occur after several days due to sepsis.*

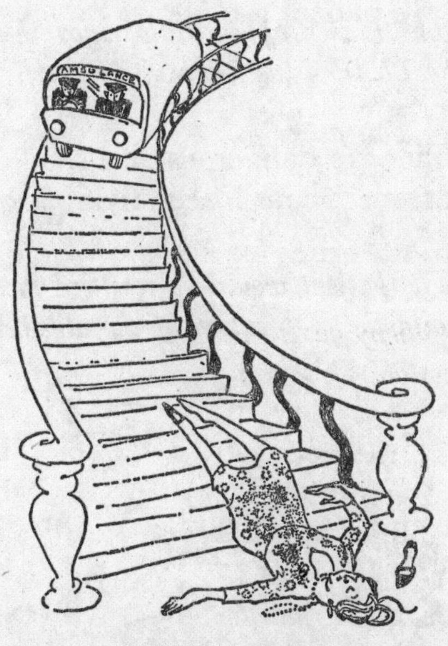


On finding an elderly patient unconscious at the foot of the stairs, an ambulance should be brought to that spot to remove her.

*I would cut the patient's trousers up the seamy side in order to gain access to the required area.*

Flies may not be easy to catch, but food should never be left uncovered in the kitchen. The fly may have just come from sitting on a bedpan to perch on the uncovered food.

*The nurses appeared to enjoy their lectures on public health from the heath visitor.*

Flies are dangerous and should be dealt with by drastic means if seen flying around the ward.

*The patient would be resettled in a satiable occupation with the cooperation of the almoner.*

*Bed spacing is arranged so that each patient has 1200 feet.*

The patient said he had been troubled by flees.

*The patient's hijeans must be dealt with regularly.*

The adult worm produces lather in the host's tissues.

The new Minister of Health is a man whose political beliefs may affect the health of his parishioners.

*Enemas are given to clean out the bowels. This is a soup and water enema. Another type is nutritional; giuen by a drip.*

A good nurse never sweats. It is essential that she uses an antiperspirant which will paralyse all her follicles.

*The freshness of the nurse determines the patients morals.*

The nurses chapel is frequently used for matings in the evenings.

## Is He Bad, Doctor?

*Straining the stool of a patient suffering from ulcerative colitis will cause perforation of the bowl.*

Constipation may be presented and the patient will often complain bitterly if it is.

*The patient was admitted to a medical ward in a state of confusion.*

The patient complained of the pain which was radiator down the arm.

*The patient was suffering from a white cell condition called lookocytoesis.*

The doctor pointed out that his patient Mrs. Church, was an interesting cuss, and the post grads should examinine her.

*The patient should be told to avoid rushing around taking things easy.*

*A patch of herpes often breaks out on the patient's laps.*

The patient was obviously suffering from heart failure because her ankles were balloons.

*The patient may develop hydrostatic pneumonia.*

If in trouble I would send for medical acid to fix the patient.

*The pulse beat may be observed in the temple.*

The onset of lober pneumonia is usually sodden.

The doctor thought that the hate regulating centre in the brain was responsible for his troubles.

*A power lass will be seen if the patient does not activate himself in his bed.*

One less common type of anaemia seen these day is known as pernickity anaemia.

As the patient was suffering from jaundice, the sister gave instructions that if the butler was used a small portion was quite enough.

*When Mrs. Patey who has been suffering from a heart condition is discharged she should be told to live below ground level.*

*The anaemic patient should have a mallow puncture, and this should be done through his stern.*

If the patient is suffering from wheel's disease he will most certainly be yellow.

*A woman's pulse is generally much quacker than a man's.*

A further complication may be due to rapture on part of the ulcer.

*The patient should be warned he is radio activated.*

The condition is extremely common in muddle aged women.

*Pyelitis occurs more readily in women than men, because the germs have fewer obstacles to surmount on their way to the urinary track.*

The ataxia of tables is very much worse after a period of confinement to bed.

*In general paralysis of the insane, the patient develops coarse tremors of the lips and hands, and argyll highlanders pupils.*

Bazaar conduct is often associated with hallucinated and deluded patients.

*The temperature of the body is the balance between hate produced and hate lost.*

Cases of the mildest forms of mental deficiency are termed feeble minded, or mormons.

*The woman was investigated and the physician diagnosed the case as one of Bill's Palsy.*

Some patients are given gold, this pleases them and their arthritis is often seen to improve.

*The patient was admitted for investigation, the fits she had been having regularly were thought to be historical and not epileptic.*

The doctor after examining Mr. Brown said he was a sack nan and needed admitting urgently.

*Sunny is the mildest form of dysentery found in this country.*

The patient's blood should be typed and criss cross matched.

*The patient often complained of musty vision.*

The doctor just walked on to the ward at 11 p.m. to do his nightie round.

*Thread worms are like small pieces of cotton when seen in the thesis in the bedpan.*

The patient's tongue was covered with furs.

THE END